The Transforming Power of a Father

By Scott Fravel

Contents

The Transforming Power of a Father

Preface

Children today find themselves in a world of confusion. It seems to them nothing is a constant, there is no one they can depend on, and there is nowhere they can go for safety. While we have many luxuries in today's world with technological advances and the availability of information, there still seems to be a lack of something in the lives of many children today. There is a key element within the family unit that seems to be decreasing year after year. The mother typically is the one who stays with the children, after all, she gave birth to them and during the early part of a child's life, the child is highly dependent upon the mother. The sad occurrence that is happening all too often is the departure of the father.

This departure may be a physical departure where the father actually leaves the mother and child and has little or no involvement in the child's life from that point forward. This could also be the result of a premature death. Another type of departure is the emotionally distant father. This father may still be married to the mother and even live in the same house as the rest of the family, but there is usually an emotional or affectionate distance between him and his children. His children grow up not really knowing who their father is and vice versa.

All of these are sad environments for a child to grow up in. On the one hand, the father is not even physically there to be with his children. On the other hand, the father is physically there, but chooses not to connect with his children. Both scenarios can cause severe outcomes in a child's life.

Let's look at the following statistics:

Children in father-absent homes are almost four times more likely to be poor. In 2011, 12 percent of children in married-couple families were living in poverty, compared to 44 percent of children in mother-only families.[1]

Data from three waves of the Fragile Families Study was used to examine the prevalence and effects of mothers' relationship changes between birth and age 3 on their children's well-being. The children born to single mothers show higher levels of aggressive behavior than children born to married mothers. Living in a single-mother household is equivalent to experiencing 5.25 partnership transitions.[2]

Infant mortality rates are 1.8 times higher for infants of unmarried mothers than for married mothers.[3]

Youths in father-absent households still had significantly higher odds of incarceration than those in mother-father families. Youths who never had a father in the household experienced the highest odds.[4]

In a study of INTERPOL crime statistics of 39 countries, it was found that single parenthood ratios were strongly correlated with violent crimes.[5]

Being raised by a single mother raises the risk of teen pregnancy, marrying with less than a high school degree, and forming a marriage where both partners have less than a high school degree.[6]

A study using a sample of adolescents aged 11 to 18 years, investigated the correlation between father absence and self-reported sexual activity. The results revealed that adolescents in father-absent homes were more likely to report being sexually active compared to adolescents living with their fathers. The analysis indicates that father absence can have a detrimental effect on adolescents' lifestyle choices. This study also revealed a statistical significance between father absence and adolescent self-esteem.[7]

Youths are more at risk of first substance use without a highly involved father. Each unit increase in father involvement is associated with 1% reduction in substance use. Living in an intact family also decreases the risk of first substance use.[8]

The National Longitudinal Survey of Youth found that obese children are more likely to live in father-absent homes than are non-obese children.[9]

A study revealed that youth who have experienced divorce, separation, or a nonunion birth have significantly higher levels of behavioral problems in school than do youth who have always lived with both biological parents. In contrast to previous GPA findings, youth living in stepfamilies or single-parent families are both more susceptible to school-related behavioral problems than youth who have always lived with both biological parents.[10]

I think by now, we can see that these findings show the importance of a father in the life of a child.

So far, I have been referring to biological fathers and the important role they play. However, you may be reading this as a step-father, grandparent or relative (in a fatherly role), adoptive father, or foster father. If that is the case, then know that your role as a father is highly important. While God's design is for a child to grow up in a family where both biological parents are there to raise him, there are many situations where the child is much better off with non-biological parents raising him, or perhaps the option of having both biological parents present is just not possible (such as the death of one of the parents). If you are a step-father, or another type of non-biological father, the role you play can still have a huge impact on the life of a child who sees you as a father figure.

If you are reading this book, then I am assuming you desire to be a better father. I am not sitting in any position of perfection in this area by any means. I have been learning as I go along in this fatherhood process. The challenge that many of us fathers face is that we don't know what the perfect example of a father looks like. How can we strive for something unless we know what we are striving for?

I had a wonderful father growing up. However, even in his many wonderful attributes, he was not perfect (sorry to burst your bubble, Dad). I think all of us can say this about our fathers.

So what is our template? Who sets the example

of what a father is to look like?

No one can fit this bill…except one. Our Father God is our example of how a father should treat his children. He sets a perfect example of what this looks like. As you read the pages of this book, I pray that Father God will reveal His wonderful fatherly attributes to you and you begin to see how you can express these same attributes in your own life to become the amazing father He created you to be. Not only will you be changed, but you will see how this will greatly impact your children and your entire family from this generation to the next. That is the transforming power of a Father!

Introduction

White. That's all I could see when I opened my eyes. I was anticipating seeing something that would give me an indication of which way was up. The saltwater stung my eyes, but it didn't matter. All that mattered was reaching the surface so I could breathe again. I felt the cut on my thigh just beneath the edge of my board shorts that was left by the fin of my surfboard, but that seemed insignificant to my lungs which were burning and screaming for air. I began swimming as quickly and as forcefully as I could in the midst of the churning sea, which resembled the chaotic currents found in a washing machine…only on a much larger scale. I was sure my head was going to erupt through the surface at any moment when it happened. As my arms reached above my head to engage in another frantic stroke, hoping this stroke would be the last one needed to reach the surface, my hands dug in…to sand. My hands were followed by my forehead scraping against the bottom of the ocean. The realization of what happened, where I was, and what I needed seemed to hit me even harder than the sand colliding with my head. I was at the bottom. I had been swimming in the wrong direction. The surface and the air I desperately needed seemed so far away. The one and only benefit to being at the bottom was I now had something to push off from. Having a clear direction of which way was up, I took advantage of this singular benefit. I positioned my feet underneath me and launched myself upward with the remaining strength I had. As my head broke free of the water and as I gasped for the life-giving air, I realized I had a lot to learn about surfing.

Years after that incident, I now find myself in a similar situation. Sometimes I feel overwhelmed at the reality of being a father. Trying to make heads or tails of a situation can take my breath away. And sometimes I find out that I have been swimming in the wrong direction! Although the more I try, the better I get at keeping my head above water. I have failed many times, but there have been those times I have emerged victorious. I have found wonderment in the joy of actually swimming instead of just trying to breathe. The Lord has shown me many things along my journey of being the father of 6 wonderful children, and I am positive that I still have much more to learn along the way. However, I do feel led to share with you my journey so far with the hopes that you might gain at least one thing the Lord has revealed to me.

Several years ago, I began my quest to understand what it truly means to be a father. There are many wonderful books available that give excellent advice and "How-To's" on fathering, but I needed something a bit deeper. I needed something fundamental about fathering. I began asking the Lord in my prayer times to show me the reality of true fathering. It was not long until Jesus pointed me to His Father. He told me to look at the interaction the Heavenly Father had with Him. So that is where my investigation began.

There are only three clear instances in the New Testament where the Father speaks to Jesus as a voice from heaven for all to hear: At the water baptism of Jesus (Matthew 3:16), at the transfiguration on the mount (Matthew 17:5), and before the crucifixion of

Jesus as He was revealing His coming death (John 12:28).

It was the second occurrence (the transfiguration) that truly caught my attention. As I began to meditate and ask the Lord to show me what was in this passage, He began to reveal to me some beautiful truths about the way a father is intended to treat His children.

I am excited to share with you this treasure of wisdom that originates from the Father. So, to all you fathers out there…enjoy the ride!

What is a Father?

Most of you who are gracing these pages are fathers. Perhaps you already have children or even grandchildren on this earth. Even if you are not biologically the father of anyone, you are still a father! Here is something to consider: if you don't currently have children, someday you may! These children might be biological, adopted, or even spiritual kids. You see, God is looking at you right now, and when He sees you He sees past, present, and future all at the same time. So, if you don't see yourself as a father right now, God sees you as being a father because He is looking ahead of where you are right now! He sees the lives you are impacting right now, but He also sees the lives you will impact in the future.

So, what does it mean to be a father? I know countless men who have biologically reproduced children and are yet to be fathers to their offspring. Being a father is much more than biological reproduction. That is the easy part! Any physically functional male can reproduce with a physically functional female to create another human being. But this physical act hardly even breaks the surface of what it means to be a father.

Many men today consider themselves fathers when all they have done is participated in the act of procreation. They are basing their fatherhood on a past event. Fatherhood is not based on a one time, past event, but rather, as we will uncover throughout this book, fatherhood is based on the "ongrowing" relationship between the male leader and the next generation.

This book is not written to discount the

importance of the mother in a child's life. Not at all! The truth of the matter is that God created man and woman, husband and wife, father and mother to be equal but different. The male in the family is designed to fill a different role than the female. Both roles are of equal importance, but both roles are considerably different. While many other books focus on the mother's role in a family and how it affects her children, this book is focusing rather on the father's role. I believe that the reason we seem to be having a decrease of true fathers in our country and in our world is because men are afraid of the investment that is required of them to truly be a FATHER.

There are many questions that come into one's mind as they begin to ponder this monumental endeavor of becoming a true father. What does a father look like? How does a father treat his children? How does a father treat his wife? Why is this so important? Who can I look to as an example of a true father?

Thankfully, we are not left without an example to follow. As we look through scripture we can see an amazing example being set for us by our Heavenly Father.

Now let us look at the story I referred to earlier in Matthew 17 where Jesus is transfigured on the Mount of Olives.

Matthew 17:1-6, NLT

Six days later Jesus took Peter and the two brothers, James and John, and led them up a high mountain to be alone. 2 As the men watched, Jesus' appearance was transformed so that his face shone like the sun, and his clothes became as white as light. **3** *Suddenly, Moses and Elijah appeared and began talking with Jesus.* **4** *Peter exclaimed, "Lord, it's wonderful for us to be here! If you want, I'll make three shelters as memorials—one for you, one for Moses, and one for Elijah."* **5** *But even as he spoke, a bright cloud overshadowed them, and a voice from the cloud said, "This is my dearly loved Son, who brings me great joy. Listen to him."* **6** *The disciples were terrified and fell face down on the ground.*

Even though this passage is only 6 verses long and the words of the Father are very few, we find great insight into the impact a Father has upon a Son. As we look at this passage a little closer you will see how the example set for us by our heavenly Father actually provides the acronym for the word "FATHER". Let's begin with the letter "F" as we investigate this complex, yet simple world of fatherhood and the ways in which a father impacts his children.

FAVOR

Matthew 17:1-3

Six days later Jesus took Peter and the two brothers, James and John, and led them up a high mountain to be alone. 2 As the men watched, Jesus' appearance was transformed so that his face shone like the sun, and his clothes became as white as light. 3 Suddenly, Moses and Elijah appeared and began talking with Jesus.

In verse 2 we see that Jesus' appearance changed. He was transformed. His face shone like the sun, and his clothes became as white as light. While all this was happening, two very important people in the Jewish culture accompanied Him; Moses and Elijah. The best way I can describe this is Jesus took on the appearance of His Father in heaven and he even got to wear Heavenly clothes which drew the attention of some VIP's in heaven. This is none other than the FAVOR of a Father upon His Son in visible form.

Peter was still talking when the Father spoke to them. Actually, the Father interrupted him…"While he was still speaking." Sometimes a Father needs to interrupt the words that others are saying about his child. If I hear somebody saying something about my child that does not match up with who my child is, then I need to interrupt and correct them. Peter was in the middle of saying something that didn't line up with who Jesus was when the Father interrupted him. Peter said, "Lord, it is good for us to be here; if You wish, let us make here three tabernacles: one for You, one for

Moses, and one for Elijah." By suggesting to make three identical tabernacles for all three of them, Peter was essentially saying that Moses and Elijah were worthy of the same amount of worship as Jesus. This is when the Father stepped in to bring correction to Peter about who Jesus was. "This is my Son, whom I love; with him I am well pleased. Listen to him!" Notice that the Father was not addressing Jesus, but the disciples! God the Father was talking to the disciples about Jesus…in front of Jesus!

A father who extends favor to his children is showing them that they are special. He is expressing their importance to him. God extends His favor toward His children all the time. The Bible regularly talks about the favor of the Lord. If you have ever experienced the favor of God, you know how wonderful it can feel to know that God will arrange things in such a way so that you are blessed, taken care of, and loved. The word favor is very similar in meaning to the word grace. So when favor is extended toward somebody, what is actually taking place is the releasing of the power of grace.

Genesis 6:8-9 says, *"But Noah found favor in the eyes of the Lord. This is the account of Noah and his family. Noah was a righteous man, blameless among the people of his time, and he walked faithfully with God."*

In Genesis 6:8 we learn that Noah found favor in the eyes of the Lord. The next verse goes on to say that Noah was a righteous man. I would like to propose that the only reason Noah was considered a righteous man was because grace was extended to him in the first place. Without the grace, or favor, of God, there is no possibility of any man being righteous on his own merit. Now you may be wondering why God would extend this favor to one individual and not to others. Why did God choose Noah above all the other people on the earth at that time to direct this flow of grace? I will also propose that perhaps God did not limit the extension of His grace solely to Noah. Perhaps God extended it to a number of individuals (or possibly even everyone), but Noah was the only person on earth who chose to be receive it!

Not only was Noah affected by this favor, but his entire family was also. God told Noah and his household (wife, sons, and their wives) to come into the ark (Genesis 7:1). The Bible never says that the other members of Noah's family were righteous. It only refers to Noah. Yet, his entire household was saved because of the favor that Noah had with God. Their salvation through the floodwaters was not based at all upon who they were. It was rooted only in the truth of who Noah was…and he was a man who found favor in the eyes of the Lord.

The story goes on to point out that God blessed Noah…and his sons (Genesis (9:1)! Again, we see Noah's sons receiving the benefit of the favor that Noah had with God. Once again, the Bible never mentions them having favor from God. Only Noah had the favor from God. So, this favor has saved them from the raging flood and it has now provided them with a blessing from God…and it doesn't stop there!

Genesis 9:8-11, NKJV

Then God spoke to Noah and to his sons with him,

saying: "And as for Me, behold, I establish My
covenant with you and with your descendants after you,
and with every living creature that is with you: the
birds, the cattle, and every beast of the earth with you,
of all that go out of the ark, every beast of the earth.
Thus I establish My covenant with you: Never again
shall all flesh be cut off by the waters of the flood;
never again shall there be a flood to destroy the earth."

Now we see God speaking to Noah and his sons describing the covenant He is making with them. This is the first covenant mentioned in scripture. Notice how the covenant is not just between God and Noah, but also with his sons…with his descendants…with the animal kingdom…and with earth itself!

Look at all that transpired from the favor Noah found in the eyes of the Lord. His entire household was saved; they were then blessed, and even established an everlasting covenant with God. This all gets traced back to the favor Noah had with God. Here is the flow of favor: Noah receives favor based upon who God is, and then Noah's sons receive favor based upon who Noah is. Even Noah's son Ham, who later proved to be someone who would dishonor his father in a scandalous moment (Genesis 9:22), received this favor.

I'm sure you remember as a child going to a friend's birthday party. The anticipation of the party ate away at your every thought for the previous 24 hours and you would be so excited to see your friends and to give the birthday boy/girl his/her present. However, as a child in our American culture there is another aspect to the birthday party that would get me all riled up. I couldn't wait until the end of the party to get THE

PARTY FAVOR! If you are unfamiliar with the party favor, this would be a small gift or bag of goodies given to all the friends of the birthday child who came to the party and typically distributed as the guests are leaving.

If you think about it, this is a very odd thing that occurs. It is the birthday boy/girl who is being celebrated, yet it is the guests who receive the party favors. What is going on here? Well, just as the name implies it is a "favor". This indicates that grace is involved. The guests are getting something that they clearly do not deserve yet it is given to them anyway. The birthday boy/girl is the only person at the party who is deserving of a gift, yet he/she has chosen to extend a gift to each of the guests.

Our heavenly Father is the only one who is deserving of any kind of gift, yet he continually pours out his gifts upon us. We are showered with His party favors every day!

As an earthly father, I have countless opportunities to extend favor to my children. Keep in mind, that extending favor to your kids does not mean you have to dish out all kinds of money to accomplish this. Often times the non-material favors that are extended toward my kids are the favors that are received the best and impact their lives the most.

During one midweek church service, I let Jadon and Hannah assist me backstage with some water baptisms during a very full water baptism schedule (they opened and closed the curtain to the baptistry and carried the participant's towels to the exit point of the baptistry). They were ecstatic to be a part of such a special event. I would not have allowed just any 6 and 8 year old to help me with this, but since they were my kids; they had favor with me and were able to participate in something that others would not have had access to.

The favor we receive from our heavenly Father is not based upon who we are, but based upon who He is. Likewise, the favor you extend toward your kids should not be based upon their merit or anything they have achieved, but simply based on who you are as their father. So, in order to extend favor that is based upon who you are, you must first know who you are (we will look closely at the topic of identity in a later chapter).

FAVOR FROM GOD

In order for a father to extend favor to his children, he must also be the recipient of favor from God. So, what is favor from God?

Favor is a special compassion of God directed toward you that creates a result through you, compelling others to like you, or work with you. The favor of God is highly attractive to others. People are drawn to those who clearly have the favor of God upon them. This creates a very unique situation because the more people who are drawn to the one with favor, the more opportunity the person with favor has to extend favor to other people.

When a father receives this favor from the Lord, not only does it draw his children closer to him, but he also gains the capacity to extend favor toward his children. If you have not received the favor of the Lord, you cannot effectively extend true, godly favor to someone else. You can't give away what you don't have.

I have heard people explain favor in this way: Favor is like being dipped in honey so that the blessings of God stick to us.

So how does someone receive the favor of God? Remember Noah? When we look at his life we see there were some stark contrasts with the way he lived his life compared to those around him. These differences are what positioned him to be receptive to God's favor. Our receptivity to grace is what translates grace into favor in our lives. So let's look at what made Noah so receptive. The Bible says that Noah was righteous, blameless, and he walked in close fellowship with God (Genesis 6:9).

First of all, he was righteous. Remember, this is God's view of Noah not man's view of Noah. God saw Noah as righteous. So, how do we get to a place where God sees us as righteous? I think Abram can help us out with this one. Genesis 15:6 (NLT) "And Abram believed the Lord, and the Lord counted him as righteous because of his faith."

I need righteousness in my life in order to position myself to receive the favor of God. And my righteousness is directly affected by my faith. If I truly believe in the Word of God and what He has told me, I am viewed as righteous by God.

A blameless life is another facet to consider when I am positioning myself to receive the favor of God. When the Bible refers to Noah as blameless, it is referring to his reputation among the other people living around him. The other people could find no fault in Noah. They had nothing to hold against him. They may not have agreed with the way he lived, or they may have even thought he was crazy, but he had done nothing to harm them or provoke them. So, just as Noah was blameless among the people who lived around him, I also need to be blameless with those who live around me. I should not be living my life in such a way that harms others or provokes them.

The final description of Noah which propelled him into the favor of God was the fact that he walked in close fellowship with God. My personal relationship with God is something that creates a receptive atmosphere for the favor of God. My hunger to know God more is a catalyst that pulls the favor of God into my life.

Proverbs 8:32-35 (NLT)

"And so, my children, listen to me, for all who follow my ways are joyful. Listen to my instruction and be wise. Don't ignore it. Joyful are those who listen to me, watching for me daily at my gates, waiting for me outside my home! For whoever finds me finds life and receives favor from the Lord."

When I find God, I receive His favor. I find him by listening to Him, watching Him, and waiting for Him. Spending time with the Lord is so crucial to the favor-receiving atmosphere that must be created in our homes.

We must realize that the time of the Lord's favor has come! We should not be waiting for another day or another time. The time is now! The favor is ready! The stage has been set! Jesus even declared that this time for the favor of the Lord had begun when he read from the book of Isaiah, *"The Spirit of the Lord is upon me, for he has anointed me to bring Good News to the poor. He has sent me to proclaim that the captives will be released, that the blind will see, that the oppressed will be set free, and that the time of the Lord's favor has come.* (Luke 4:18-19, NLT) Then He said, *"The Scripture you've just heard has been fulfilled this very day!"* (vs. 21).

COMMITMENT

Commitment is another aspect of favor that is important to a child. It is important for a child to know that his father is committed to extending favor to him. Oh the damage that occurs to a child when they don't know if dad is going to be there for them or not. The uncertainty that this brings into the relationship is extremely damaging. When a child does not know if he can count on dad being there to help him, to encourage him, to pour into him, to console him, to instruct him, to protect him and provide for him, it creates a lack of self-worth in the child. If a child sees himself as less important than the other things in the father's life, he has a hard time seeing his significance in the world.

When my children know they have daddy's favor, they have the sense that they can accomplish anything. Because daddy's got their back! They know that daddy sees them through eyes that keep them elevated over others. In other words, when I see my kids, I don't just see kids, I see MY kids! They are no one else's kids. They are mine. I am the only daddy they have on this earth. I have an important role to play in their lives. No one else can play the part that I play in their precious, God-given lives. I have opportunities all the time to extend favor to MY kids. Not because of what they have done, but because of who I am in their life. I am Daddy! As Daddy, I have the ability to make choices that my kids cannot make. So, this concept of favor actually involves choice. As I extend favor to my children, I am showing them that I am choosing them over all other things I could choose from. When my son looks at me and I extend favor to him, it is as if I am saying, "I choose you!" That is the favor of a father.

"I am your father, and I choose you!"

AFFECTION

Matthew 17:4-6

Peter exclaimed, "Lord, it's wonderful for us to be here! If you want, I'll make three shelters as memorials[a]—one for you, one for Moses, and one for Elijah."
5 But even as he spoke, a bright cloud overshadowed them, and a voice from the cloud said, "This is my dearly loved Son, who brings me great joy. Listen to him." 6 The disciples were terrified and fell face down on the ground.

In this passage, we see that the Father not only referred to Jesus as His Son, but His Son whom He loves. How powerful is that? Remember, the Father is declaring this to others, and Jesus is hearing the words of His Father. So, the Father is publicly sharing the AFFECTION He has for His Son by publicly declaring "I love You."

Unfortunately, there are many fathers today who have never told their children that they love them. While hearing those words of affection is a powerful moment for any child, there is something even more powerful when that proclamation is heard when it is addressed to others. Remember in this scenario, the Father was not addressing Jesus; He was talking to the disciples.

While my father told me many times that he loved me, one of those times that stands out from the rest was my wedding day. During the reception, my father spoke some very kind words to Ruth and me and we were very blessed by those words. However, there was one thing in particular that really stood out to me. When he told the entire crowd that had gathered at our reception of his love for me and how proud he was of me. It is one thing for a father to tell his child this in a private intimate setting (which is important as well), but it has a unique impact when it is stated publicly. Many people assume the sole responsibility for meeting the need of affection in a child's life falls upon the mother. While the mother is an excellent source of affection for a child, it should not be the only source. A child desperately needs the affection of a father in his life as well.

Philippians 1:8, NIV

God can testify how I long for all of you with the affection of Christ Jesus.

   In Philippians 1:8, we see the apostle Paul, acting as a spiritual father, telling the people at the church in Philippi that his affection for them is the affection of Jesus. This word used for affection is the Greek word "splagchnon", which refers to the inner bowels of a person. The bowels were regarded by the Hebrews as the place where the tender affections resided such as: kindness, benevolence, compassion, etc... So, Paul was saying that the way Jesus feels about them is the same way he feels about them. He is allowing the affections of Jesus to flow through him and be directed toward this group of people whom he considers his spiritual children.
   I daily try to tell each of my children the

affections I have for them. I use words and actions that put on display and reinforce these affections. I don't ever want my kids to wonder or question how I feel about them. I will use different words to express my feelings with each of my kids based upon which child I am speaking to, as well as what is currently going on in their lives. A child should never be uncertain about the feelings his father has towards him.

The Lord even lets us know that this is how a father should treat his children. In Psalm 103:13, it says, *"The Lord is like a father to his children, tender and compassionate to those who fear him."* When it says the Lord is "like a father", God is telling us that this is how a true father "should" act toward his children. There are few times in scripture where it says the Lord is like something else. He is so different than everything else (He is holy), that there is usually no comparison at all. However, here we see the word of God describing God in this way. It is comparing God to a father. There is an expectation in this verse that fathers are to treat their children with tenderness and compassion. When that expectation is met by an earthly father, then his child will recognize the heavenly Father by these same qualities because that is what God is like too.

One day, my oldest son, Jadon, was having some difficulty with some of the other boys at his school. They were using their words to make fun of him and tease him. Not surprisingly he came home quite upset that day. His head was lowered and his shoulders were hunched over. I saw the defeated look on his face as he looked at me. I quickly gathered him into my arms and let him share with me all that happened to him that day.

After giving him adequate time to share with me the details of the situation, I lifted up his chin, looked into his eyes and shared with him the affections I had for him. "Jadon, you are so special to me," I said. "I love you so much. I'm so sorry that those things happened to you today, but always know how much I care about you. That will never change. What those boys did was wrong and they should not treat you that way. But I'm so glad that their thoughtless words and actions cannot change the way I feel about you."

His face visibly changed at that moment, and although I can't say that it made everything completely better for him at school, he obtained a sense of peace at that moment knowing that situations may shift, and people may treat him good or bad on different days, but through it all, his dad will always love and care for him.

God even reminds us of His affection toward us by the quantity of thoughts He is constantly having about us.

Psalm 40:5, NKJV

Many, O LORD my God, are Your wonderful works
  Which You have done;
  And Your thoughts toward us
  Cannot be recounted to You in order;
  If I would declare and speak of them,
  They are more than can be numbered.

The affection a father displays is important not only when it is directed toward the child, but also when it is directed toward the mother. In other words, the affection a father displays toward the mother has a great impact on the child. Even in a divorced situation, when the father shows appropriate affection in the form of love and respect, this can have a huge impact on the child.

A father's affection directed toward his daughter is of utmost importance. It is during the early years of her life that she is shown what affection looks like between a wife and husband. She is always observing and remembering how her father treats her mother. These observations then begin to form a standard of which she will regularly compare other men in her life. This standard eventually plays a principal role in her choice of a husband.

She is also constantly absorbing the ways in which her father treats her directly. If a young girl is treated poorly by her father at a young age, whether by ridiculing, slander, demeaning words, physical/mental/emotional/sexual abuse, she will most likely be drawn to that in her future relationships. If her father was non-existent (meaning that her father was not around during her early years) she more often than not will grow up having a difficult time connecting and being open with her own husband.

I am constantly looking for ways to express my affections toward my daughter. Hannah loves it when I spend time with her; tell her how pretty she is, and how much I appreciate her loving ways with her brothers. She also gets really excited when she sees me and Ruth give each other a hug and a kiss. When I show my affection for my wife in front of my daughter (appropriately of course), Hannah's expression is priceless. She will acquire a look on her face comprised of a conglomeration of expressions including: surprise, happiness, embarrassment, and a grossed-out look on her face. It is obvious to me that she is really touched by this display of affection and it is definitely making an impact on her life. Even though she is acting as if she is grossed-out by our displays of affection for each other, there is something else there that tells me she loves to see it, because deep down she knows that the affection I am showing toward my wife is real and beautiful.

CONSISTENCY

One summer day in 2012, we joined our friend Joe who lived in an area with a community pool. Joe and I decided it would be fun to teach my kids how to do cannon balls into the pool. Joe walked to the edge of the pool and yelled, "Cannonball!" as he jumped in to make a gigantic splash. I followed with, "Cannonball!" as I created a tsunami of my own.

The kids learned quickly and soon one after the other they began jumping into the water to create their own miniature tidal waves. They also repeated what we said as they jumped in..."Cannonball!" screamed Jadon. "Cannonball!" squealed Hannah. "Cannonball!" proclaimed Joshie. And then bringing it up the rear, "Santa Claus!" squeaked Judah. I realized that Judah (he was 3 years old at the time), did not so much care about what he was saying as much as saying what he thought needed to be said. He said it with the same enthusiasm as everyone else who yelled "Cannonball." Even when our kids don't get it quite right, our hearts melt toward them as they do their best.

While that story is cute and adorable, not all situations are quite as easy to show our affection toward our children. Consistency in attitudes, behavior, and affection is paramount to a child's intimacy with his father. If a father is affectionate one moment, and then the next moment, he is distant and untouchable, it sends mixed signals to the child, and the child never knows if daddy can be approached or not. This creates an uncertainty within the child that threatens the very relationship between father and child.

In moments of correction and/or discipline, it can be extremely difficult, even painful, to express our affections toward our kids. It is during those times, that our kids must see the affections we have for them. So, when your child breaks that china plate on the ground, or is throwing a temper tantrum because they didn't get as much ice cream in their bowl as their sibling, it is those moments that we need to reassure them of our affection for them even if correction and/or discipline is necessary too.

Affection should always be extended to your child no matter what the situation. If your child notices that your affection for them does not change as a result of their actions or words, they find a sense of security knowing that dad will always love them even when they mess up. This is a reflection of our Heavenly Father's love for us. It is unconditional. The love that God has for you is not dependent upon your actions or your words. He loves you with an everlasting, unchanging, intense love that is extended to you in every situation, whether you mess up or not.

Not only does God love you, but His thoughts about you are countless! He is a father who is always thinking of His children. *"For the Lord delights in his people... "* (Psalm 149:4, NLT) His affections for His children are innumerable. *"... Your thoughts toward us cannot be recounted to You in order; if I would declare and speak of them, they are more than can be numbered."* (Psalm 40:5, NKJV)

That is how your heavenly father thinks of you. That is your example of how you are to be thinking of your own children. You are to be thinking of them constantly. You are to be thinking of them with good things in mind all the time. It is when our thoughts are regularly upon our kids that we can come to a place of full affection towards them. A place where our hearts burst with joy, kindness, gentleness, and love for those little ones who are in desperate need to experience this kind of affection.

"I am your father, and I delight in you!"

TRUTH

The world we live in is full of all kinds of information, suggestions, opinions, thoughts, philosophies, ideas, and lies. Not only is our world saturated with all these, but our kids are constantly bombarded with them wherever they go! One of the major problems with all of these different thoughts, ideas, etc. is that often there is some kind of agenda or lie that is interwoven within it. Children today can hardly go anywhere without some kind of agenda being crammed down their throats.   So, how are our kids supposed to navigate through this toxic sludge of "modern thought" without being conformed to the world? Scripture tells us that we should not be conformed to this world, but be transformed by the renewing of our minds (Romans 12:2). There is something going on in our minds that has a huge impact on whether we are being conformed to the world or whether we are undergoing a mind transformation. What is it that affects our minds? Truth.

Matthew 17:4,5

Peter exclaimed, "Lord, it's wonderful for us to be here! If you want, I'll make three shelters as memorials—one for you, one for Moses, and one for Elijah."
5 But even as he spoke, a bright cloud overshadowed them, and a voice from the cloud said, "This is my dearly loved Son, who brings me great joy. Listen to him."

Note that the Father saw it necessary to bring correction to the disciples. These three individuals misunderstood what they were seeing in the scenario that was playing out before them. When they saw Jesus talking with Moses and Elijah, they jumped to the conclusion that Jesus and the other two impressive beings were equal and on the same level of worship. The Father could not let this misunderstanding go on any further... He let the TRUTH be known.

Referring to Jesus, He spoke to the disciples letting them know who Jesus really was. He was revealing truth to these three characters. When the truth was released into this situation, the lie (that Jesus, Moses, and Elijah were equal) had to leave.

Truth is the one thing that can overcome lies. When lies are presented with the truth, they cannot stand. When darkness is exposed to light, it must flee. The questions then arise...what is truth? How do I get it? Pontius Pilate asked this question to Jesus. Before Jesus died on the cross, He stood before Pilate and Pilate asked the very poignant question, "What is truth?" This is a core question that must be asked by everyone who is seeking answers. What is truth?

John 14:6

Jesus answered, "I am the way and the truth and the life. No one comes to the Father except through me."

Jesus is the truth. That is the answer. It is as simple as that. If we want to know truth, we need to know Jesus. If we want to know the Father, we must go through Jesus.

All the way back in the book of Genesis, we see how God created the heavens and the earth and how He dwelled among men. Adam and Eve had the privilege to walk with God in the cool of the day. His very presence was physically manifested here on the earth with man. That is how God originally intended our planet to function...as the place where God and man dwelled together. However, it did not stay that way.

When Adam and Eve sinned, they not only invited death into this world, they also caused God to remove His presence from this world. God immediately set in motion a plan to remedy this awful situation. He knew what had to be done, and He began the work right away. He deeply desired to have His presence live among man again.

His plan was to send His only Son, Jesus to take care of sin once and for all. To make the payment that must be made. The Father sent His Son and that is exactly what happened. Jesus took the sins (past, present, and future) of the entire world upon his shoulders and made a payment that we couldn't make. He then conquered death, hell, and the grave through his resurrection. After His resurrection, He told His disciples that He must leave them so that He could send the Holy Spirit.

Look at the progression: The Father sent the Son. The Son sent the Holy Spirit. And now the Holy Spirit leads us back to the Father. How does the Holy Spirit do this? By using truth. John 16:13 *"But when he, the Spirit of truth, comes, he will guide you into all truth. He will not speak on his own; he will speak only what he hears, and he will tell you what is yet to come."*

The Holy Spirit leads us into truth. He speaks

what He hears the Father saying to Him. As we give heed to the Holy Spirit's words, we can't help but draw closer and closer to the Father.

Fathers today have an enormous responsibility to guide their children into this truth. It is through this guidance that children will obtain the skills and discernment needed to make the appropriate decisions in life based on truth and not based upon any lie or agenda the world or the enemy is trying to throw at them. But that is not the only benefit from this truth encounter. The father, as he seeks the truth to share with his own children, is drawn closer to the heavenly Father himself. If you have ever preached a sermon, prepared a Bible study, or anything similar, you probably have noticed that whatever you are preparing for is just as much needed by you as it is by the people you are preparing to share it with.

Truth is something a father must obtain first before he can possibly share it with his children. As fathers, we must recognize that truth exists whether we know it or not. When I gain knowledge about something, I have uncovered and received a certain amount of the truth that already existed even before I received it.

Proverbs 22:12, NLT

"The Lord preserves those with knowledge, but he ruins the plans of the treacherous."

A father must be constantly speaking the truth he has received into the lives of his children. Not opinion, but truth. It is not wrong to share your opinion with your children, but you must also present the truth. In other words, it is OK to tell your kids that you don't like something or you disagree with something that has taken place. However, you must also let them become increasingly aware of the superior truth that exists in that same situation. "I don't like this, but the word of God says....." The truth must always be recognized as superior to any opinion, concept, or thought. My opinion without the truth creates prideful superiority. My opinion with the truth reveals humble inferiority.

By displaying the superiority of real truth in your own life, you teach your children that truth is what rules and reigns in your life. And as your children become more and more familiar with real truth, they will become closer and closer to Jesus. As they become closer and closer with Jesus, they become closer and closer to the Father. How does that work? Jesus said, "He who has seen me has seen the Father."

INTEGRITY

It is when truth reigns in the life of a father that other qualities of a father shine through. For example, integrity. The definition of integrity is: the adherence to moral and ethical principles; soundness of moral character; honesty.

The only way to display "honest" character is to embrace the truth. You must tell the truth in order to be honest. You cannot embrace a lie and still be honest.

Even the entire concept of faith is based upon truth. The faith I have in salvation is based upon the truth of what Jesus accomplished on the cross and His resurrection from the dead. If something proves to be untrue, then it is impossible (or at least illogical) to put my faith in that.

Truth is something that affects many aspects of the relationship between father and child. That is why it is so important for dads to always be seeking after the truth, drawing closer to Jesus, and as a result coming closer to God the Father. It is through my relationship with God the Father that I truly learn how to be a good father.

HUMILITY

Another quality that is dependent upon truth is the silent and powerful characteristic of humility. A father must remain humble when faced with truth. Without humility only pride can exist, and pride has been well known and documented to destroy individuals, families, cultures, and countries.

Proverbs 13:10 (NLT)

"Pride leads to conflict; those who take advice are wise."

When someone is full of pride, they don't feel that they have need of others in their life. They feel very independent and make the false assumption that they have all the answers. As we grow older, we typically grow wiser, and one phrase that has always stuck with me is, "When I was in high school, I thought I knew everything; now I realize I hardly know anything."

Coming to the realization that others can help you out in life is a humbling experience and humility is needed to avoid many conflicts in life. In a healthy person, wisdom and humility should grow together as we get older. Unfortunately, many people act as if there is a reverse correlation between the two and as they get wiser, they think they should become more prideful. The more wisdom I gain as I get older, the more I realize how dependent upon God I truly am. When a child sees his father grow in wisdom and humility, it sets the stage for the child to grow in these areas as well. You can't be a prideful man and expect your child to grow up humble.

Without truth a child ends up wandering aimlessly through life, grasping at anything that provides some kind of answer or solution no matter how trivial, superficial, or meaningless it actually is. However, when a child receives the truth, this child now has the opportunity to walk in wisdom! When a father sees his child walking in wisdom, it brings much joy to his heart. How do you know if your child is walking in wisdom? Let's allow the book of James to show us what that might look like:

James 3:13-17

"If you are wise and understand God's ways, prove it by living an honorable life, doing good works with the humility that comes from wisdom. But if you are bitterly jealous and there is selfish ambition in your heart, don't cover up the truth with boasting and lying. For jealousy and selfishness are not God's kind of

wisdom. Such things are earthly, unspiritual, and demonic. For wherever there is jealousy and selfish ambition, there you will find disorder and evil of every kind. But the wisdom from above is first of all pure. It is also peace loving, gentle at all times, and willing to yield to others. It is full of mercy and good deeds. It shows no favoritism and is always sincere."

A child truly becomes established and rooted in the truth when their father is speaking truth into them and living truth around them.

"I am your father, and I will teach you."

HONOR

Matthew 17:5 NLT

"This is my dearly loved Son, who brings me great joy... "

The New King James Version says, *"This is My beloved Son, in whom I am well pleased... "* These words carry an impact in a child's life like no other. Remember, in this scene, the Father is speaking to the disciples who are looking on in amazement at what has transpired in front of them. The Father has already shown His favor toward His Son through the transformation, He has expressed the love that He has toward His son, and now He moves on to recognize, acknowledge, and approve of the actions carried out by this son whom He loves by sharing His thoughts about Jesus to those who are listening.

One of the power sources within a family unit is honor. It is an area so pivotal in affecting the way individuals in a family treat each other that it can almost be viewed as currency. I am not suggesting that we use honor to buy things in our relationships, but rather to use honor as a source of investment.

When we utilize our money with the future in mind, we do what is called investing. We willingly put our money into stocks, bonds, mutual funds, 401K's, or other forms of investment with the hopes that this money will grow into something even greater in the future. There is always a risk factor involved when investing and some investments are more risky than others.

Honor can be viewed very similarly. Instead of money, we invest honor. Not into banks, or bonds, but into people. Our natural tendency is to withhold honor from those who appear different than us or act different than us. But it is through honor that true freedom is found. As Danny Silk explains in his book *Culture of Honor*, "Honor is one of the most vital core values for creating a safe place where people can be free. Honor protects the value that people have for those who are different than they are."

When a father honors his child, he is letting his child know that he is thinking about his future. The child will grow up with the sense that his dad thinks that his future is worth investing in. Honoring another person is basically bringing the very quality of the kingdom of heaven into the situation and upon the other person. Honoring your child is communicating, "This is what heaven is like, and I want you to have some of it right here, right now...because you are worth it! Your future is worth it."

CHOICES

One powerful way to extend honor to a child is to always give them a choice. My wife, Ruth, and I have adopted some very helpful tools on raising kids that we picked up from the parenting organization, "Love and Logic." One skill they teach constantly is to give your child a choice. By providing your child with a choice, you engage him in the outcome of the situation and allows him to be a part of the solution. He also learns that he actually has the ability to make choices, whether good or bad.

Now, when our children are young, we typically give them a choice between two options we can live with. In other words, it doesn't really matter to us which option they choose, because we are completely satisfied with either choice. It may look something like this: When we are nearing the child's bedtime we will simply ask, "Judah, do you want to get ready for bed right now, or in five minutes?" We are perfectly satisfied with either answer and we commend them for making such a great choice, no matter which option they choose. Another example: "Hannah, would you like to wear your pink shirt or your purple shirt today?" Once again, we are completely satisfied with either of the choices and our daughter has now engaged in the decision making process.

What is happening in this situation is that the child is learning some very important decision making skills that seem to be lacking in many children today. As they grow, they will need to make decisions from other options not presented to them by their parents. Anytime a child gets to make a decision in the context of a safe and loving family, it is a good thing! This is because whether or not it is a good or bad decision, they get to make the decision, and then they get to deal with the outcome of that decision, whether good or bad. The great thing about teaching this to your children when they are young, is that the consequences are so much smaller during these early years. "Love and Logic" actually teaches the parent to look forward to the child making bad decisions when they are young, because they will learn from it. The hope here is that they will make fewer bad decision when the consequences are more sever a few years down the road.

When our oldest son Jadon was in Kindergarten, we began to implement this parenting approach. The school where he was attending was not close to our house at the time, and it took about 25 minutes to drive to the school. We had instructed Jadon that he needed to be ready to leave at 7:50 am in order to make it to school on time. During his morning preparation, he got distracted (like many kindergarteners do) and lost track of time because of all the fun he was having playing with his toys. When 7:50 am rolled around, I grabbed my things and declared, "It's time to leave." Jadon looked at me with horror on his face and painfully stammered out, "But I still have my pajamas on!" I replied, "Well, that is so sad that you chose to wear your pajamas to school today." I gathered him up, placed him in the car and drove him to school. He spent the entire day at school in his pajamas. As I was driving him to school, Ruth called his teacher and explained what was happening. She was more than willing to play her part in helping Jadon learn this lesson. Jadon was not allowed to play at recess because he was out of his dress code that was required of all students at his school. That was probably the worst part for him.

Was that decision difficult for me to make? Yes! My first impulse was to help him get his clothes on for school and scold him for not getting it done in time. Thankfully, I refrained from following that course of action. Was it difficult for Jadon to receive? Yes! The screaming and crying during the entire 25 minute drive confirmed that much. Did Jadon learn to make better choices during his morning preparation? Yes! Even to this day, when he wakes up in the morning, he makes his bed and gets dressed immediately.

Providing options and giving them opportunities to make a decision is a powerful way to extend honor to your children. By allowing them to make a decision, you are essentially saying to them, "You have a choice in front of you right now. You are perfectly capable of making this choice on your own. So whatever you choose, I will completely honor you. And you get to deal with whatever the outcome of that decision might be. But I will honor your decision."

When a child receives honor from their parents, it is extremely powerful. They begin to realize that their decisions matter, that their thoughts, actions, and words matter. Too many kids are ignored by their parents today. They are not allowed to make their own decisions and therefore never learn to do so because their parents have always made all the decisions for them. Parents who make all the decisions for their children create children who make poor decisions.

"It is typical, for example, when a teenager begins to explore his or her freedom, that his or her parents become afraid. The fear stems from the fact that the child is choosing options that the parents either wouldn't ever or wouldn't again choose for themselves. The wrestling match is over how different the child can be so as to individuate from the parents and how much the parents can keep the child looking like them. The further the child moves from how the parents live, the more likely the parents are to step in and shut down the child's choices. The result is conflict. But when the teenager and the parents both practice honor, which contains within it love and trust, fear is not allowed to rule their decisions and freedom can be preserved." - Danny Silk. [11]

Honor also strengthens the family all around. Here is why: people will tend to gravitate to the place where they receive the most honor. If you don't honor your children when they are young, then when they become teenagers or older, they will not have much of a desire to be around the home because they have learned that "home" is not where they are honored. This is one of the main reasons that teenagers begin to get involved with gangs or attach themselves to other unhealthy associations. They are honored in the gang, so that is where they want to spend their time.

Children, that are constantly disrespected at home, ridiculed and talked down to by their parents, will typically spend less and less time around their home as they grow older until eventually they don't come around the home at all and become estranged from their parents. All of this could have been avoided by simply extending honor.

DISCIPLINE

Disciplining your child is one of the most important ways you can bring honor to a child. "Bringing honor to my child through discipline?"- you may ask. Absolutely. The fifth of the ten commandments tells me that I must honor my father and mother. Therefore, I must help my children understand what this looks like by extending honor to them first. After all, how does a child know what honor looks like unless it is demonstrated to them first?

Most children experience a dishonoring form of discipline. Often times it is merely a form of punishment. There is a big difference between discipline and punishment. Punishment is typically applied through an attitude of resentment, anger, or frustration and is meant to administer atonement for a poor decision. This typically results in the child's emotional state descending into fear, guilt, or shame. On the other hand, discipline is applied through love and concern and is meant to train and correct the child to become a mature individual who can make wise decisions. This typically results in a sense of security and honor for the child. Children should be brought into alignment with God's commands through correction and discipline because they are worth it.

Proverbs 3:12

"For whom the Lord loves He corrects, just as a father the son in whom he delights."

I have seen a situation unfold time and time again in a public scene. It usually goes something like this: A parent and child are in a supermarket or theater, or perhaps at a park or in a parking lot (name your public place). The child makes a poor decision and the parent obviously gets upset. The parent then decides that their current location is as good a place as any to administer a form of discipline. Now, sometimes discipline needs to happen immediately and swiftly. But many times it does not. In fact, we have seen tremendous results in the "delayed consequence" approach. If our children make a poor decision in public, instead of administering discipline at that very moment I will simply say, "that is so sad you chose to make that decision, looks like we will have to deal with this when we get home." The benefit to this approach is that it gives the parent some time to think about what appropriate disciplinary action is needed and it also gives the child plenty of time to contemplate what they have done. The obvious challenge for the parent in this situation is following through with the discipline when you get home!

Unfortunately, when I encounter the before mentioned scene, the typical response from the parent is one that does not bring about the desired effect. The parent usually gets visibly angry and yells at the child. The child already knows he did something wrong and the parent is now just venting his/her anger at the child to help make themselves feel better. Because of the heated situation they have a hard time seeing the relationship between them and their child break down right in front of them.

When a parent disciplines out of anger there are extreme negative consequences upon the child. When a parent disciplines out of love the results are much different. God the father shows his perfect love towards us when he disciplines us, so we as fathers should show that same love towards our children. When we experience anger from our disciplinarian, it is a wide open door for the spirit of fear to come in. When we experience love from our disciplinarian there is no opportunity for fear to come in and there is a wide open door for the relationship to grow in love and honor. When we have experienced the perfect love of God, we are not afraid of Him. When we have not experienced it, we become afraid of being punished by Him.

1 John 4:18, NLT

"Such love has no fear, because perfect love expels all fear. If we are afraid, it is for fear of punishment, and this shows that we have not fully experienced his perfect love."

When honor is built upon truth, the results can be great. A child, who grows up being taught the truth, will be able to obtain knowledge from this truth. As the child grows, this knowledge also has the potential to grow into wisdom. Wisdom is the ability to utilize knowledge to make sensible decisions. You can't have wisdom without knowledge. A parent, who helps his child see the truth of a matter, provides the child with knowledge, which can then turn into wisdom when applied correctly. Wisdom is a crucial element in a child in order for them to receive discipline.

Proverbs 13:1, NLT

"A wise child accepts a parent's discipline; a mocker refuses to listen to correction."

Disciplining your children is needed but children should not be provoked in the process. When you discipline, do it in such a way where extending honor back to you is not a huge challenge for them. The discipline should change them but it should not change the way they feel about you. If you expect your child to honor you, show them what honor looks like. Honor them in how you discipline them. That does not mean that you refrain from discipline or you go easy on them but rather you do it in such a way where they are not embarrassed or shamed through the process but honored.

Ephesians 6:4, NLT

"Fathers, do not provoke your children to anger by the way you treat them. Rather, bring them up with the discipline and instruction that comes from the Lord."

PRAISE

Praise your children openly, reprove them secretly. - William Cecil (16th century English statesman)
As a parent, I must always take the time to celebrate my children. I must celebrate them in the big victories as well as the smaller accomplishments. Sometimes the accomplishments are intentional and other times they are accidental. However, there are opportunities to extend honor in all of them.

One day as our family was sitting down for dinner, I sat across the table from our 3 year old, Judah. He has been instructed many times not to stand on his chair, but apparently he was still trying to remember this lesson. Now let me inform you that our dinner table is not a standard height table. Nope. In fact, it is quite a bit taller than most tables. The chairs are almost the height of bar stools. The flooring under our table is hard wood floor which makes for easy clean-ups when the kids spill their food or drink (notice I said "when" not "if").

As we sat down for dinner, I noticed Judah standing on his chair in his jeans and t-shirt reaching for an item on the table (I don't recall what the item was, but it is irrelevant to this story). He had a very focused look on his face, determined to acquire the item on the table. It happened when he was about mid-reach. His foot somehow slipped off the chair and he fell to the side. I saw his head disappear below the top of the table and then I saw one of his feet fly up in the air. I don't know if I fully understood the physics behind this maneuver, but somehow his feet came up and his head went down. Since I was on the opposite side of the table, I couldn't do anything but yell out, "Judah!" I was expecting to hear a loud thud as his head hit the hard wood floor, but the sound never manifested. By this time, I was already trying to make my way over to the other side of the table to comfort my son and to see if there was going to be some serious damage to his poor little head. Before I even got to him, I heard his small little voice say, "Daddy, I'm doing a handstand!" As I rounded the corner of the table I noticed that his other foot had caught his momentum underneath the lip of the table's edge which enabled him to somehow keep his balance as his hands landed squarely on the ground. He was in fact performing a most excellent handstand. He was actually quite proud of himself.

I was amazed at how a terrifying event (for a 3 year old…and for his father) turned around and was able to become a moment of achievement for him instead. We celebrated with him for this disaster-avoiding achievement and he realized that he was honored through something that could have ended up with much different results.

Instead of harshly bringing criticism upon him we chose to honor him by celebrating his achievement. He was clearly a bit shaken up by the experience, and had already learned his lesson about standing on the chair. There was no need to get upset or angry at this little guy who obviously did not want to try it again. Honoring your child through a potentially heated situation can do wonders to strengthen your relationship.

TIME

Another form of honoring your children is by listening to them. By sitting down and giving your child your undivided attention as they share something with you, you are honoring them by demonstrating to them that the words they want to share with you are worth your time, which also means that "they" are worth your time.

If you haven't discovered this already, when you spend time with your kids, you will uncover questions within yourself. Sometimes these are questions you have suppressed for years or even decades. They are the questions that you would rather not address, or have ignored for a particular reason. Other times they are questions that you have never even considered before. Maybe you pondered about this topic or line of thought before, but you have never been able to phrase the question in such a way as your child before you just

---

did. When you give your child an opportunity to speak into your life by bringing up some tough questions, you are honoring him/her. There have been times our children have brought up a question without even saying any words at all. Sometimes they just use their actions. Many times it is their actions that speak louder than words. In fact their actions can even scream!

There have been several times (ok, more than several) when my kids have asked me questions that I don't know the answer to. When these questions are spiritual in nature, it draws me to seek out the answers from my heavenly Father. By honoring my kids and allowing them to pose challenging questions, it has actually driven me closer into the arms of my Father as I seek the answers. Spending time with your kids reveals many questions; spending time with God reveals many answers.

When a father spends time with his children he is investing time into the next generation. Why is this important? Because the next generation is going to take things further than we have ever gone before.

"I am your Father, and I will honor you."

EMPOWERMENT

Matthew 17:5

"...Listen to Him."

At this point in the Father/Son encounter, the Father then finishes His already powerful statement with one last portion that places Jesus in his rightful place of authority. "Listen to him" are the words the disciples heard just before their faces hit the dirt. With just these few little words, the Father has done something wonderful and needed in the life of His Son. The Father has empowered His Son. He has just let the disciples know that they must listen and obey the words that Jesus shares with them.

I have counseled many people who live their lives in bondage to fear and anxiety. Fear that something bad is going to happen or the anxiety arising from something that has already happened or is about to unfold. They seem to always have the worst-case-scenario in mind. When I get down to the root of when this all started, many times I find they have never felt protected from their father when they were a child. This lack of protection opened them up to the spirit of fear that has controlled them ever since.

The needs that God has designed to be met within the family unit by the father are the needs of protection, provision, and identity. These three needs have been designed by God to be primarily met by the father. Let's first look at the need of protection.

Protection

Imagine a complete family unit. Now imagine a five year old boy playing outside in the front yard while mom and dad are doing some long awaited gardening on the side yard. While the child is playing with his toys and having a great time, up strolls the neighborhood bully who decides he wants to destroy the little boys toys and even do some harm to the boy. Knowing that mom and dad are just several feet around the corner, who do you suppose the child will run to for protection? It's Daddy! Why? Because God created the family unit in such a way that dad is the primary person to meet the need of protection for the children. That is what dad does. He protects. There is safety in the arms of a father. At least there should be.

Matt 2:13

An angel came to Joseph in the dream and said, "Get up! Flee! Someone is trying to destroy your son!"

An angel had come to Mary before to tell her of the soon coming birth of the Messiah through her own womb. Through this meeting, we know that Mary was highly receptive to angelic encounters. So, why then did the angel not come to Mary again to tell them of the threat toward their son, Jesus? After all, doesn't a mother want to protect her child just as much as the father does? The angel did not come to Mary because Joseph was the earthly father and as the earthly father, it was Joseph's responsibility to provide protection for his son. This does not mean that a mother cannot protect her children. She absolutely can, and should. However, it is not her primary responsibility as a mother. It is the father's primary responsibility to meet this need of protection in the life of his children.

While children need physical protection provided by their father, the protection of a father does not just stop with physical protection. Just as in a battle scene where a shield or armor is needed to protect a combat soldier physically, a father must be the shield for his children mentally. The enemy knows that the battlefield is in the mind and this is where he regularly attacks us.

Continually helping our children renew their minds is such a crucial ingredient to raising children who are full of life.

Romans 12:1, 2 NKJV

"I beseech you therefore, brethren, by the mercies of God, that you present your bodies a living sacrifice, holy acceptable to God, which is your reasonable service. And do not be conformed to this world, but be transformed by the renewing of your mind, that you may prove what is that good and acceptable and perfect will of God."

There are times when a child seeks out the protection from his father. However, there are other times that a father needs to extend protection when the child does not realize he needs it, or even when the child does not want it. There will be times in every father's life when there is a need to protect his child from various threats whether it is physical, mental, emotional, or spiritual.

Every father must constantly be leaning into the Holy Spirit to hear what He is speaking into the heart of the father at that moment. There are times when a father needs to intervene to extend protection for his child. However, there are other times when the father needs to let the child experience the harshness of life and unfortunately "learn the hard way."

I am one to extend the protection initially to all my children. If my children receive my protection and learn that I am there to help them, not to harm them, then I can keep extending my protection to them knowing that they are learning to trust in me and will eventually understand the reasoning behind my decision.

However, if my child continually rejects my protection even after I have proven that my protection is there to help him, not to harm him, I will eventually allow him to leave the protection of my covering (depending on the situation). What typically happens is the child learns the hard way. What he learns is that my protection is there to help him through life. I don't want my child's future to be destroyed or ruined in any way because I was not there to provide the protection a father needs to provide. Sometimes, I'll step in to protect my child from a harmful situation, but one that my child does not want me involved with. I will simply look at my child and say, "I love you too much to ruin your tomorrow." They may not understand exactly what that means at the moment, but someday they will.

So how does protection fit in with

---

empowerment? I'm glad you asked. When a child does not have a sense of protection, he tends to shy away from the adventures in life. God has given each one of us different combinations of gifts and abilities that He intends us to use. If a child does not feel safe, he will not explore the gifts and abilities God has given him. These wonderful treasures will remain locked up and hidden in the "back closet" of their life because he is afraid that if he tries to use it something bad might happen.

A father is there to help uncover and reveal who the child is (more on this subject in a later chapter). When a child feels protected and secure in what God has given him, he is ready to go out and face the world with the gifts and abilities God has given him. This is empowerment, and protection plays a key role in it.

Provision

The second need a father is uniquely designed to meet within the family unit is the need for provision. A father makes sacrifices in his own life so that his children have their needs met and more. Unfortunately, many fathers don't realize there is a wrong way to provide for their children. When you take all the credit for being the provider, you are doing your children a disservice. They need to know their needs are ultimately being met by God. Always giving praise and glory to your Heavenly Father will demonstrate to your children that you are dependent upon God and they should be dependent upon Him too.

As a father, you should be a reflection of God's

provision in the lives of your children, and as you provide, you should consistently direct their focus back to your Heavenly Father who is the ultimate provider. This will provide a sense of security in this area of provision which then empowers the child to move forward in life boldly knowing that their Heavenly Father will always be with them to provide their every need.

If a child learns to solely be dependent upon his earthly father, then when he grows up and moves out of the house he will feel like he still needs to be dependent upon his earthly father. What happens when tough times hit? They come, running back to daddy. But, if a father demonstrates to his children that even as a father he is dependent upon God, what a different path the kids will take from that! When tough times hit, instead of running to their earthly father, they run to their heavenly Father. This is how we should be directing and training our kids to respond in these situations. Consider these verses:

Isaiah 38:19, NCV

*The people who are alive are the ones who praise you. They praise you as I praise you today. A **father** should tell his children that you **provide** help.*

Matt 6:8, NLT

"...For your Father knows exactly what you need even before you ask him!"

Matt 6:32, NLT

"...Your heavenly Father already knows all your needs."

Can you see the effect this has on empowering your child? He needs to grow up knowing that his earthly father is meeting all his needs, but it is really the heavenly Father who is working through his earthly father. And even though his earthly father won't be with him his entire life, his heavenly Father is going to be with him through everything! Not only will He be with him, He already knows all his needs and is ready to meet them!

Inheritance

Providing for our children is important in the here and now, but we should also be thoughtful about providing for their future. We must do what we can during our time with our kids while they are young, but there will come a day when they will not be under our care anymore; either they will grow up and move out, or we will not be living to provide for them. King David gives us an example of what this looks like.

In 1 Chronicles 22:8 God tells King David that he was not going to be the one to build the temple unto God because he had "shed much blood." Instead, David's son Solomon was the king chosen to build this magnificent temple. Living in the twenty- first century we have excellent hindsight as we look back upon this event and we can see the crucial role David played in all this.

Even though David was not chosen to build the temple, his role was foundational in what Solomon was able to accomplish. First of all, David's role as king was not to build the temple, but to acquire the land for God's people to dwell in. God knew that land would be required in order for His people to live in safety and for an environment to exist where this glorious temple could be built.

Secondly, David's role was to obtain the resources needed to build the temple. This included not only the physical material but some of the primary craftsman that would be needed to achieve the quality of work required for such a project.

2 Chronicles 2:7, NLT

"So send me a master craftsman who can work with gold, silver, bronze, and iron, as well as with purple, scarlet, and blue cloth. He must be a skilled engraver who can work with the craftsmen of Judah and Jerusalem who were selected by my father, David."

David had desired in his heart to be the one to build the temple, but the Lord told him, *"You wanted to build the Temple to honor my name. Your intention is good, but you are not the one to do it. One of your own sons will build the Temple to honor me."* (1 Kings 8:18, 19 - NLT)

Note that God told David that it was good that it was in his heart to build such a thing. So, David realized that he still had a part to play in this majestic project. So, he spent much of his last years on earth building up the resources and materials needed for the construction of the temple. He even contributed in many of the plans for the temple. He orchestrated things in such a way so his son, Solomon, would be successful in this grand project long after David was gone. And Solomon was very successful in building this magnificent temple unto the Lord.

As fathers, we must realize that not only does God want us to do great things in this world while we are here, but we are to leave an inheritance to our children so that they can continue to do great things long after we are gone. One of the viewpoints I have adopted in my life is that I desire to live my life in such a way that I have taken the Fravel family (including past generations) further than we have ever gone in our walk with the Lord before. However, the other part to that viewpoint is to orchestrate things in such a way that the pinnacle moment at the end of my life becomes the platform for my children to launch from so they can take it even further than I was able to!

Providing for your children includes the here and now, but it also extends into the future even long after you are gone.

Opportunities

I can remember as a child how my father would always provide for me. We were not a super-rich family, but we were able to live in a very nice, safe neighborhood in Northern California, have our bills paid, and really enjoy life without being burdened with a lack of finances.

Not only did my father provide for his family financially, he also provided for us in many other ways.

One particular way that he seemed to enjoy providing for my sister and me was to provide us with opportunities. We had many opportunities placed before us and it was up to us to decide what to do with those opportunities.

In 1990, in San Jose, CA, when my sister, Jill, was 16 years old, my parents were kind enough to purchase her first car for her. For only $1500 they were able to purchase a red and white 1956 Chevrolet 4-door hardtop 210 (it looked very similar to the Bel-Air model, just with 4 doors). It needed a bit of work inside and out, but it ran just fine on the original engine.

Two years later, my sister left for San Diego to go to college. I was sad to see my sister move away, but I couldn't have been happier to discover that she was not taking her car with her! I turned 16 that same year and immediately acquired my driver's license. By default, I became the primary driver of this classic car! Without missing a beat, I quickly began assuming responsibility for the car. I talked with my dad about what could be done to the car to improve upon it. We enjoyed researching all kinds of options together.

Finally we decided to put a new (actually rebuilt) 350 engine inside the Chevy. I was extremely excited about this, but I had no idea how to do it. So, my dad, our good friend Richard, and I worked hard and placed this new engine inside the Chevy. It was through the process of installing a new engine in this car that I learned a great deal about cars and how they work. I am still not a car expert, but I sure did learn a lot during that time. But it was only because my dad provided me with an opportunity that I was allowed to grow in this area.

One of the worst things a parent can do to a child is to remove opportunities from them. It is through the opportunities that a child learns, grows, and experiences. Empowering your children through these opportunities is an amazing opportunity for you too. Encouraging your child is a significant part of empowerment. Your child needs to hear from you that you believe in them, that you think he has what it takes to accomplish this task or make it through this particular situation. This is extremely meaningful to your child.

In the 2003 computer-animated film entitled *Finding Nemo*, there is a great lesson to fathers about letting their children take advantage of opportunities. The film is about a clownfish, Marlin, who is on the search for his son, Nemo. During his search he befriends a regal tang, Dory, who helps to shine some light on his perception of fatherhood. After Nemo went missing, Marlin and Dory began their search for him as this scene unfolds:

Marlin: I promised I'd never let anything happen to him.
Dory: Hmm. That's a funny thing to promise.
Marlin: What?
Dory: Well, you can't never let anything happen to him. Then nothing would ever happen to him. Not much fun for little Harpo.

The first time I took Jadon fishing, it was so much fun. To see the anticipation in every action as we prepared for our trip was almost as much fun as the trip. When we got to the lake, I took out all our fishing gear and showed him what all of it did. Then I prepared his fishing pole and made the first cast for him to show him how to do it. I handed him the pole and the biggest smile crept across his face. After a while, he reeled in his line (a little too fast due to his excitement) and proceeded to hand me the pole to cast it for him again. I looked at him refusing to take the pole from him. He looked back at me with a look of "what do you expect me to do?" I said to him, "Go ahead. Cast it yourself." The realization hit him all of a sudden and the expression on his face said, *I am supposed to make the cast all by myself this time*! A small nervous laugh escaped through his slightly parted lips. Then he stuck out his chest a bit and held the fishing pole behind him to wind up his throw, then, he swung his arms forward to launch the line as far as he could. The only problem was that he didn't release the line, so the line just swung out from the pole about two feet, just dangled there, and didn't unwind at all. He looked at me with a quizzical look on his face that said, "What went wrong?" He wanted to hand the pole back to me so I would cast it for him. I refused once again. I gave him some additional instruction on making a successful cast and he listened attentively realizing that if he were to ever make a successful cast today, he would have to pay close attention to the instruction I was offering him at that moment.

It still took him several more tries before he made his first successful cast, but when he did; his excitement was through the roof! What he experienced was empowerment. Empowerment is void of judgment and condemnation, but is filled with opportunity and encouragement.

Freedom to fail

Another crucial element within empowerment is failure. When I empower somebody, I must recognize and accept the likelihood that they will fail sometimes. Failure does not always happen initially, but often times it does. What our society has grown accustomed to is the protection from failure. This has hindered the growth of our children in a detrimental way. One of the most effective ways we learn is through failure. So, when we remove the ability to fail, we also remove the ability to learn.

Once again I refer back to what my wife and I learned through Love and Logic. The consequences of failure at a young age are much milder than they are when they become older and the consequences become much more severe. I would much rather have my son suffer the consequences of a small failure when he is young than to witness the consequences of his failures as an adult, which always seem to have more serious consequences. Of course, empowerment does not demand failure. Sometimes failure is the way it starts out, but the hope is that they get to the place where they experience victory in a particular area. Every failure is temporary, but every victory is eternal.

An interesting story unfolds in Genesis. Abraham was given a promise; *"You'll be the father of many nations. Your name will no longer be Abram, but Abraham, meaning that I'm making you the father of many nations. I'll make you a father of fathers—I'll make nations from you, kings will issue from you. I'm establishing my covenant between me and you, a covenant that includes your descendants, a covenant that goes on and on and on, a covenant that commits me to be your God and the God of your descendants. And I'm giving you and your descendants this land where you're now just camping, this whole country of Canaan, to own forever. And I'll be their God. And Sarai your wife: Don't call her Sarai any longer; call her Sarah. I'll bless her—yes! I'll give you a son by her! Oh, how I'll bless her! Nations will come from her; kings of nations will come from her."* (Genesis 17:4-8, 15-16, MSG) Sarah did indeed give birth to a son in her old age and they named him Isaac. He was the son of the promise.

Here is where the story takes an unforgettable turn. Everything seemed to be heading down a great path, but then God asked Abraham to kill his son that this promise would come through! I'm sure at some point Abraham told Isaac all about God's promise, so Isaac was not ignorant of the situation. We see great faith in Abraham's willingness to let his son go (sacrificed), because he believed the Lord's promise that a great nation would come through Isaac.

We also see Abraham empowering his son Isaac to walk in the promise of God, in spite of the physical appearance of the situation. Abraham, could have stepped in the way and prevented any harm to come to his precious son, but instead, he allowed Isaac to carry the wood and fulfill his role as this surreal scene unfolded before him. Likewise, as fathers, we must believe the Lord's promises about our children and be willing to release them into those promises.

One summer day in 2012, my son, Judah, almost drowned in a pool while we were visiting my wife's family in San Diego. I went out surfing early that morning enjoying my time at the beach. On the way back to the house from the beach, I got a call on my cell phone from Ruth. Immediately I could tell she was panicked and obviously shaken at the first sound of her voice. She shared with me how Judah (3 years old) jumped into the pool with no adult around. Thankfully, our oldest son, Jadon (9 years old) was near and jumped in and tried holding Judah's head above water. Ruth soon saw what was happening, ran, and jumped in the pool fully clothed to pull Judah to safety.

When a parent goes through a life threatening situation with one of their children, it cuts them to the core. They once again realize how precious life is and the horrible thoughts begin to run through their head about the "what if's". Imagining life without a child is a very difficult thought to have. Actually going through it would be an entirely different matter. For those parents reading this book who have lost a child, whether the child was still young or whether they were an adult, my heart goes out to you. Because it is your own flesh and blood. This is life that came through you and is physically no longer with you.

I hope and pray that I never have to experience that. But I have close friends who have lost children, and I have seen the pain on their faces. Each time I encounter a family who has lost a child it is a huge wake up call to me about parenting and the short opportunity a mother and father have to pour into their kids while they are young. I don't want to lose a single moment during my kids' childhood. I need to constantly be looking for ways to pour into them and teach them while they are young because there will come a time when I have to let them go and that will be a difficult day. But I hope and pray that when that day comes, they will be ready to make all the right decisions that they need to make in life and I have prepared them and empowered them to the best of my ability. At that point, I must leave them in the hands of the Lord.

"I am your father, and I will empower you."

REVELATION

Matthew 17:5

"This is my dearly loved Son..."

In order to understand this concept of Revelation, we have to backtrack a bit in this encounter with the Father and Son. We addressed this statement in the chapter on Affection, but within this statement is more than the Father just telling the Son of his love for him. There is something that is obvious, yet overlooked in these brief words. The Father was making a public statement about Jesus. In this public statement, the Father gave an example to all fathers today. The Father REVEALED the identity of Jesus by saying, "This is my Son." The Father declared the relational truth that existed between Him and Jesus. He was not just saying that Jesus was a special man, a prophet, a king, a priest, or the messiah (although Jesus was and is all these things too). He was declaring the relational reality that existed between the two.

You can imagine the countenance on the disciples' faces when they heard this voice from heaven. It is pretty clear that their faces must have been filled with expressions of fear, shock, and awe, because it says, *"And when the disciples heard it, they fell on their faces and were greatly afraid."* Not only did their visage show fear, their bodies demonstrated it by falling face down on the ground.

I can remember as a child on countless occasions when my dad would take me out (either to a store, to his hometown of Santa Cruz, or to his work) and very intentionally introduce me as his son. It would go something like this, "Hey Mike, it's great running into you here. I haven't seen you in years! Let me introduce you to my son, Scott." It was that last statement that invited a surge of joy into my life. My dad could have easily carried on a conversation with that person without ever acknowledging me, but he chose to make it a point to let that person know that I was there, and that I had an intimate relationship with my father because I was his son.

Romans 8:19, NLT

"For all creation is waiting eagerly for that future day when God will reveal who his children really are."

In this verse, we see what God the Father is going to do with his children. He is going to reveal who we really are! That is His heart. The word "reveal" means to uncover or to make known. His desire is to make known to all of creation who His children really are! That is the heart of a true father...revealing the true identity of his children.

If we, as fathers, are to be reflecting God the Father and taking notes on how He treats not only His Son Jesus, but all of His children, then it would stand to reason that our desire should be similar. You should desire to reveal to the world who your children really are! Your children can only begin to see who they are when you start revealing it to them...when you start uncovering them...when you start making them known.

While most of us are familiar with the traditional concepts of the father being the protector and the

73

provider, there is another need that has gone largely unattended by fathers in our society…the need for identity. Fathers oftentimes ignore this area of identity and instead have replaced this with the concept of independence. So, instead of uncovering the true identity of his child, the father allows the identity of his child to become inward focused and wrapped up within themselves.

When a person bases his own identity on how he sees himself, it can create an ever fluctuating sense of identity. Our feelings change, our understanding changes, and our circumstances change all the time. If our identity is rooted in these aspects of our lives, then our sense of identity is in a constant state of flux, and we never really know who we are at any given time.

Our true identity is not wrapped up in ourselves, but it is completely enveloped in who God is. I am "me" because God is God. Without God, there would not even be a "me." Therefore, the fundamental aspect to my own identity is completely fused to the existence of God and who He is! The identity of anything created is anchored in the one who created it! A car is known by what company made it (Ford, Honda, BMW, Mercedes, etc…). A coin is known by what country made it. Likewise, humans should be known by who made them.

The father is the member of the family who is responsible to begin this revelation process concerning the true identity within each of his children. His children should grow up knowing their true identity.

Identity

Our country is dealing with an identity crisis. I believe that one of the fundamental reasons our country is in this state today is because we don't know who we are. While it is correct that we don't know who we are as a country, it goes even deeper than that. We don't know who we are as individuals. There is such a lack of identity in this world it is amazing we can get anything done on a regular basis!

The United States of America is a wonderful country. It is based upon states that are united. Our states are built upon counties that are united. Our counties are built upon cities that are united. Our cities are built upon neighborhoods that are united. Our neighborhoods are built upon families that are united. It is the family unit that is the foundational unit of our country. This is why the devil makes families such a huge target in his efforts to "kill, steal, and destroy."

The enemy desires to wreak havoc on the family unit which will in turn wreak havoc on neighborhoods, cities, counties, states, and ultimately our country and then the world. He knows that if the families are destroyed, the rest of the world will follow. This is so true and we can see the impact it has had on our world for the past several decades, if not longer.

One of the basic needs a father provides for his young children is the need for identity. The father provides this through the process of revelation. Revelation is the uncovering of something previously hidden. Each child has a unique identity. It is the father's responsibility to begin to uncover the identity that is within each of his children.

I remember when I was a young child playing

little league baseball. It was so fun to get out there on the baseball field, throw the ball around and hit it as hard as I could. One of the things I will always remember is when my dad would come to my games. He made most (if not all) of my sporting events even though he was a very busy man, and somehow he would make the time to come to my games and sometimes even my practices.

While I would be playing a game, I can remember looking toward the stands for my dad. If I hit the ball really good when I was up to bat, (which was not all that often) I would always look toward the stands. Sometimes I would see my mom there cheering me on. She would be saying, "Great job, Scott!" I would be very thankful that my mom was there to cheer me on, but she was not dad. When my dad would be there somehow things just seemed different. I would look to the stands after that good hit and he would say the exact same thing, "Great job, Scott!" But when it came from my dad, it had a different meaning behind it. Here is why: the father is the person who is designed to reveal the identity within the child.

Identity is solidified through affirmation and encouragement. So, when my dad yelled, "Great job, Scott!" What my soul was hearing was, "I am so proud of you. You are someone special. You are on the right track. Keep it up! I love who you are becoming!" When I would see my dad cheering me on, somehow I would puff out my chest a bit more and feel more confident and bold in who I was and what I was doing. It's funny, because his words weren't any different than my mother's words, but when they came from my dad, those words would speak directly to my identity.

Unfortunately, many children today are struggling with their identity. Here are some real life prayer requests taken from our church's youth group (teenagers) that have to deal with their identity:

I am lost. Pray for me.
Pray that my father and I are able to connect.
I need help to know that I'm beautiful, not ugly.
My life feels like it is spinning out of control.
I can't see my beauty, unless I hear about it.
I worry about whether or not I should eat every day.
I don't know how to forgive.
I treat my little brother like he is worthless, and I hate myself for that.
Anger towards my dad.
I am depressed.
I feel so alone and unwanted.
I need God to bring me something to help, a miracle, His voice, I need him to show me He is here.
I need a prayer for my family to stop fighting.
I want my tender, innocent heart back.
I feel stifled by my parents.
I'm home alone alot…stressed and becoming depressed.
I need prayer to know that the cops won't show up at my house.
I need prayer so friends stop making fun of me.
I need prayer for my attitude.
Pray that I treat my brother better, like I should.
My mood changes on a dime. Only God can help me.
I'm lost.
I don't know what I'm doing anymore.
Sometimes I know exactly what to do but other times I

just don't see my way in and out of things.
I don't see worth in myself.
I feel useless and that I have no point.
I see myself as ugly and fat.
I feel and treat myself like crap.
I don't know how to express my feelings.
I'm feeling overwhelmed.
I have anger towards myself and others.
Pray for my family. We all fight and argue. I wish things would get better.

Raising my own kids I am very aware of the identity that I am speaking into them. When speaking identity into my kids, I like to use a simple tool often times utilized in book reviews or research analysis. It is asking 6 little questions: Who, What, When, Where, Why, How.

WHO

Who am I? This is a question that has plagued countless people throughout history. It is a prime question of importance because the answer to this question directly affects ones thoughts, actions, and destiny. For instance, if my answer to that question is: "I am no more than an evolved, conglomeration of matter that has no real purpose other than to occupy this place in space and time so that the next level of evolution can come about", then my thoughts will be based upon this concept which will direct the actions I choose, which directs my destiny. That answer will lead to thoughts such as: "I have no real significance. I don't really matter to anyone. There is no point in me being here. Why even try to live a good life, it doesn't matter in the end anyway." It doesn't take much imagination to figure out what the following actions would look like. Extrapolate those actions into the future and you can easily determine someone's destiny which is all based upon the answer to that simple question, "Who am I?"

Man has been given "free will" which allows us to make decisions that affect our destiny. We even get to plan our own course!

Proverbs 16:9

"In their hearts humans plan their course, but the Lord establishes their steps."

The answer to this question is of utmost importance. Identity is a key element that has been significantly replaced with the component of independence. When my identity is based upon who God is and my relationship to God, much can be said about my dependence on Him rather than my dependence on myself (independence).

At the Jordan River, Jesus was baptized in water by John the Baptist, which marked the beginning of Jesus' earthly ministry. When Jesus emerged from the waters of the Jordan River during his baptism, his Father called from heaven and said, *"This is My beloved Son, in whom I am well pleased."* The Father spoke identity into the Son. He told Jesus who He was! Jesus was able to go forth and begin His ministry empowered by the identity that was spoken into Him by

His Father. A father stands in the unique position to speak identity into his children that no other person can occupy.

Luke 6:35-36, MSG

"I tell you, love your enemies. Help and give without expecting a return. You'll never—I promise—regret it. Live out this God-created identity the way our Father lives toward us, generously and graciously, even when we're at our worst. Our Father is kind; you be kind."

Even in the Old Testament, there is reference to this:

Psalm 2:7 (NLT)

"The king proclaims the Lord's decree: 'The Lord said to me, "You are my son. Today I have become your Father." "'

A father tells his child *who* he is. I regularly ask my children this question and I love to hear their response. One night as I was tucking my daughter, Hannah, into bed I asked her (she was seven at the time), "Hannah, do you know *who* you are?" She looked at me and said with a crooked smile, "Daddy, of course I do. I am a princess." I probed a little further, "What makes you say that you are a princess?" She replied, "Because my Father is the King." I couldn't help but get a bit choked up when she shared this with me. I was so glad that she was recognizing and accepting who she is. She said the truth when she said that her Father is the King. She IS a child of the King! It was wonderful to see that she has already begun to recognize her identity and that her identity is wrapped up in who her heavenly Father is.

Sadly, we see an example in scripture of what happens when a father fails in this area. King David had many wonderful qualities, yet he did not bring revelation to his sons about who they were.

Ultimately, this led to rebellion and fighting over the throne. The throne became the focus of their lives and they thought their identity was found in the throne (power). The throne became so important to them that they were willing to fight each other for it…even willing to fight their father David for it. Without the throne, they felt their identity was shattered, so they were willing to risk it all to obtain the throne…their (false) identity.

Many parents today teach their children similar things all the time. Their children grow up thinking that if they don't have power (physical strength, economic power, intellectual power, etc…); they are not significant in this world. Many children grow up today thinking that their identity is wrapped up in these things.

In 1 Samuel 2, we see Eli doing the same thing to his sons.

"Now the sons of Eli were scoundrels who had no respect for the Lord or for their duties as priests. Whenever anyone offered a sacrifice, Eli's sons would send over a servant with a three-pronged fork. While the meat of the sacrificed animal was still boiling, the servant would stick the fork into the pot and demand

that whatever it brought up be given to Eli's sons. All the Israelites who came to worship at Shiloh were treated this way. Sometimes the servant would come even before the animal's fat had been burned on the altar. He would demand raw meat before it had been boiled so that it could be used for roasting." (vs. 12-15)

Eli may have been a prophet of the Lord during that time, but he obviously failed at being a father to his children. By the time his sons became priests, they came to the conclusion that their identity was wrapped up in their position as a priest. When our earthly position becomes more important than our heavenly position, we lose sight of who we really are.

WHAT

Following the "who" question, I usually then ask another question. "What are you?" The first question answered the fundamentals of who she is. She is a child of the King. That is true and that will never change. The "What" can also change and in many cases should be changing, that is, growing. One area that the "what" deals with is the character qualities of an individual…their attributes. For instance, I may be a child of the King—"who"— (1 John 5:1), but I am also courageous—"what"— (Psalm 31:24). I may be a joint-heir with Christ (Romans 8:17), but I am also reverent (Philippians 2:12).

The whole design of biological reproduction plays an important role in the identity of a person. For instance, you get your unique combination of chromosomes, which are made up of DNA molecules that determine all of your physical features of your body and many other aspects of you as well, from your biological parents. The moment a child is born (even earlier through the technological advancement of ultrasound); this individual is immediately placed into one of two categories that will forever be a part of their earthly identity. The child is either male or female.

This is an aspect to the "what" question, and an obvious one, because it is a physical quality that we are all familiar with. We see it on forms that we fill out all the time. A typical form will ask you some basic information about yourself: your name, address, phone number, email. But often times, there is another piece of information that many companies or organizations will require from you, and that is your gender. They want to know whether you are male or female. This is an unchanging aspect that gives further description to the "what" question. We know this because if I were asking someone over an email about their gender, I would not say, "Who are you, male or female?" I would not ask it that way, because it is not addressing the "who" question. Rather I would ask, "What are you, male or female?" This is because it more clearly answers the "what" question about an individual. This is one of the most fundamental "what's" of each person who has ever existed.

Here is something that confirms the role the father plays in identity. At the moment of conception, it is the father, not the mother who determines the gender of the child. Through the sperm, the father contributes either an X chromosome (female) or a Y chromosome (male). So, right from the start of this new life, the father (albeit unknowingly) is already speaking identity into his child! God set it up that way. He set something in motion He never intended to be changed. The father is the intended parent to speak identity into the life of his children.

WHEN

This leads into another question. "Do you understand the time in which you are living?" This fulfills the "when" question. I try to lead them into understanding the time in history in which we are alive, the challenges that we face today, and the God who we serve that is still the same yesterday, today and forever.

Jesus was constantly reminding his disciples of the times they lived in and the times that were to come. He was preparing them (and us) for the future so that we might not be caught off guard. (Matthew 24, Mark 13, Luke 12, 21) Our children need to be aware of the special time in history that they live. They need to know that God chose them to be alive on this earth "for such a time as this."

One summer, Jadon and Hannah attended a summer soccer camp. Joshua was pretty bummed that he could not go to the soccer camp. Josh is pretty athletic with whatever sport is presented to him. But the kids needed to be at least seven years old to attend this particular soccer camp. Josh was still five at the time. I grew up being the youngest sibling (I only have one sister who is older), so I know how it feels to get to do everything last. I think Josh was feeling this way.

He feels that Jadon and Hannah always get to do

things before him, and they do! They were able to go to this camp before he could, they get to have sleepovers at their friends' house before he does, they will get to drive cars before he does, simply because they are older and they will always reach a certain age before Josh will reach it. I'm sure we will deal with these same feelings with Judah, Josiah, and Jeremiah as they get older, too. The challenge as a parent is letting each child know how special they are even if they are too young or short at the moment.

Part of a parent's responsibility is to train a child to be excited for every moment in life. Because as we get older we look back on our childhood and realize how fast it went by, and how we wish we could go back to the simplicity of childhood. There was such an easiness to it that is hard to imagine obtaining right now. However, we need to still have simplicity activated in our lives even as adults.

A child's life is a reminder of how simple our lives should really be. We often times fill our lives with so many things that when you think about it, we can really live without. If all I had to worry about was being too short or too young, that would be fantastic! I'll take it! We have many other issues in life that we deal with now, don't we? Now, it is a matter of being too heavy, or being too old or too poor or too unsatisfied. Our kids pick up on this. They are more observant than we give them credit for. If I show my dissatisfaction in life and I complain about everything happening all around me, guess what my kids will be doing? You got it. They will find it pretty easy to head down that same path because you have already paved the way in that direction. They will complain, and become dissatisfied with everything happening in their lives.

As a father I need to be sure that I am showing excitement and satisfaction to my children in all areas of life. I am not saying that I pretend or that I ignore difficult situations. On the contrary, I can address difficult situations as my children are looking on and taking mental notes. They see dad going through a tough time, but instead of getting mad or upset at everything and everyone around me, they see me saturated in the peace of God, keeping a cool head and a positive outlook on life, knowing that my God is bigger than my situation. That is what they will learn from and grow from.

WHERE

The "when" question easily leads into the "where" question. I try to explain to them that wherever they are, whether they are at school, at home, at the store, or playing with friends, that they have opportunities to glorify God.

Psalm 119:54, NLT

"Your decrees have been the theme of my songs wherever I have lived."

2 Corinthians 3:17 NLT

"For the Lord is the Spirit, and wherever the Spirit of the Lord is, there is freedom."

A father shows his child where he lives and where to go. I usually start with the big picture. Looking at the whole universe and then zeroing in on planet earth is a good starting point (a good visual representation can come in handy). From there I gradually help them to focus more clearly on where they are: continent, nation, state, city, neighborhood, church, school, family. When they see that they are in a specific place in all of creation and God wants to do something wonderful through them in this place, it excites them to try to find it out.

After helping my children see where they live, I also like to see what other areas God has placed on their hearts. Sometimes children will share that they have a special love for a certain type of people group that live in another part of the world. This can be very revealing and demonstrate a possible call to be a missionary or to do some other kind of foreign missions work. We can then begin to prepare them for where God might be taking them in the future. Or perhaps, your child will reveal a heart for people who are in the inner cities which may lead to some kind of urban work.

Remember, your children will not be living in your homes forever, and there will come a time that their "where" will change. As parents we need to do all we can to prepare them and then send them into the "where" God is calling them.

Our heavenly Father knows what it is like to send His Son. *"Furthermore, we have seen with our own eyes and now testify that the Father sent his Son to be the Savior of the world."* - 1 John 4:14

WHY

The "why" question is always a fun one for me. Ultimately, the reason we are all here on this earth is to glorify the Father. Jesus knew why He was here on earth, *"...I have come that they may have life, and that they may have it more abundantly."* John 10:10 (NKJV). Also in 1 John 3:8 (NKJV) it says, *"he who sins is of the devil, for the devil has sinned from the beginning. For this purpose the Son of God was manifested, that He might destroy the works of the devil."*

Paul also gives us the answer to this "why" question in Ephesians 1:12-14 (NLT) *"God's purpose was that we Jews who were the first to trust in Christ would bring praise and glory to God. And now you Gentiles have also heard the truth, the Good News that God saves you. And when you believed in Christ, He identified you as His own by giving you the Holy Spirit, whom He promised long ago. The spirit is God's guarantee that He will give us the inheritance He promised and that He has purchased us to be His own people. He did this so we would praise and glorify Him."*

The reason why your children are here is not to get a paycheck or even obtain happiness. While the "where" may change throughout their life, the "why" never changes. In everything we do, no matter what we do, when we do it, or where we do it, we are to bring glory to our heavenly Father.

This can be brought into perspective for them in all the little things they do. They go to school to learn and equip their minds with knowledge so that they can use that knowledge to bring God glory. They clean their rooms so that they show how grateful they are for what God has given them and bring Him glory by taking care of it. They treat their family and friends with love, kindness and respect because they recognize that each person is a precious life that God created, and treating His creation this way brings glory to Him.

If your kids have not received salvation by asking Jesus into their hearts, this is a great way to introduce the gospel message to them. You can explain to them that everyone has sinned and because of that sin, it has separated us from God. There is nothing we can do to close that separation, and God knew it. So, God sent His one and only Son to close the separation by making a payment for all our sins. Now, because of what Jesus did on the cross, we can have a wonderful relationship with our heavenly Father once again if we simply receive Jesus as our Lord and Savior. Bringing Him glory is the only appropriate response after all He has done for us.

HOW

The "how" question gives great practical ideas of what all of this might look like when applied to their life. It is a great time to share with them some of your own experiences, the victories and the failures.

We bring glory to God by living lives that are pure. *"God has called us to live holy lives, not impure lives."* −1 Thessalonians 4:7

We bring glory to God by living lives that resemble the life of Jesus. *"Those who say they live in*

God should live their lives as Jesus did." - John 2:6
We bring glory to God by living holy lives without fear and full of righteousness. *"We have been rescued from our enemies so we can serve God without fear, in holiness and righteousness for as long as we live.*" - Luke 1:74-75

We bring glory to God when we live our lives filled with faith. *"For we live by believing and not by seeing*" – 2 Corinthians 5:7

We bring glory to God by living lives that are moral and generous. *"You can be sure that no immoral, impure, or greedy person will inherit the Kingdom of Christ and of God. For a greedy person is an idolater, worshiping the things of this world.*" -Ephesians 5:15
Helping your children to see their true identity is one of the most important things for a father to instill in his children's lives. When they realize their identity, it positions them to be launched into the calling that God has placed on their lives.

"I am your father, and I will reveal who you are."

BE TRANSFORMED

It is interesting that when a child is learning to swim, the most important thing is keeping your head above water so you can breathe. However, once that is under control, the most important thing is going from point A to point B...getting from here to there...and, of course, having fun in the process. There is no sense teaching a child how to get from one side of the pool to the other if they can't keep their head above water.

I believe as a father of young children, it is important to teach them early how to keep their head above water in the world. What does that mean and what does that look like? Keeping your head above water in the world is really one of the foundational aspects of life. If I know who I am and why I am here, I am keeping my head above water. Despite all the negativity the world throws at me or lies the enemy tries to hurl at me, I know who I am and I won't drown in the corruption that surrounds me. Instead, I learn how to easily keep my head above water and how to get from point A to point B all while enjoying the journey that is in front of me.

A father has an opportunity to show their child what this looks like on a regular basis. When faced with a trial or a challenging moment, the child is looking on with wide eyes waiting to see how father reacts to this situation. If a father lets the situation overwhelm him and pull him down, the child sees his father drowning, not enjoying the journey. The child also loses all aspects of forward progress, too. He doesn't know where point A was and he definitely doesn't even care about point B. He sees his father flailing about, drowning in this thing called life, and it gives the child no hope for his own life. After all, "if my amazing dad can't handle the things of the world, how can I?" But if a child sees instead a dad who does not let the things of the world pull him down, but able to keep his head above water, this has an entirely different effect on the child. First of all, the child does not feel like he has to save his father. Secondly, the child realizes that the cares of the world, while important, should not be what affects our peace or joy in life. Also, when the child not only sees his dad keeping his head above water, but also enjoying his time in the water even though the route from point A to point B may have changed, the child will grow up knowing that when trials and tribulations come, he does not have to let it pull him down. Instead, he can realize that there is something greater than the things of this world. The peace we carry does not need to be dependent upon the world around us.

I am always amazed when I watch the Olympic Games. These games contain the best of the best athletes. One of the amazing sports that is so fun to watch is the swimming competitions. It is amazing how fast those athletes can swim in the water (Michael Phelps comes to mind). Also, there are various strokes that are utilized in different competitions. There is the freestyle, breast, back and butterfly stroke. Then there is a competition called the medley where they swim all four strokes during the race! This is quite a feat!

Children need to see their fathers swim a medley. In other words, they need to see what it looks like to utilize different strokes during different situations. One situation may call for a back stroke, while in another situation the breast stroke may be more effective.

One of the fun things about surfing is that you have to pick and choose your wave. There are several factors that play into this decision. Size of the wave, your location with respect to the wave, your energy level at the time the wave is approaching, and other surfers that might be in your area are some of those factors.

Since moving to Colorado, I had not been surfing in several years, so my current experience is not what it used to be. That is something I had to take into consideration in the summer of 2012 when we went on a family vacation to San Diego, CA. There were a few larger waves that approached me that I chose not to take, because I felt that my current experience level would not be sufficient to handle that kind of wave. However, I did attempt some waves that stretched me beyond what I believed my current skill level to be.

There were a few waves I would have liked to ride, but my current location with respect to the wave would not have allowed me to take it. So I sat by as other surfers enjoyed those rides. Obviously it was not a wave for me.

Also, my energy level played a part in this. My body has not been use to paddling through the surf to get into surfing position. So I was using muscles that I had not used regularly in quite some time. After paddling through the surf and getting into surfing position, there were times when a great wave came by and I had to pass on it. Why? Because I had nothing left! I was drained and knew that I would have no energy to paddle to catch the wave.

Also there were times when I would be poised to

catch a wave, I had plenty of energy, but another surfer took it first. Instead of getting upset and letting it ruin my day, I found myself getting excited for the other surfer and the opportunity he had to ride that wave. After all, not all the waves are for me.

As a father I need to teach my kids many lessons that can be learned through surfing. Waves are like opportunities. Some should be taken, and others should be let go. But how do you determine which wave to ride and which one to pass on? There are opportunities in life that will come your way that are much too big for your current situation. And if you decide to take it, you may soon find yourself going through the washing machine of life getting tumbled around every which way. You may want to pass on them instead.

Sometimes there are opportunities that are just too far out of your reach with respect to where you currently are (not just geographically, but emotionally, spiritually, educationally, or occupationally). You may put all your effort to try to achieve something that you are not in a position to go after, and not only will you miss that opportunity because you are not positioned for it, but sometimes you take yourself out of position for the next wave that you should have taken.

We also need moments of rest in our lives. If I try to do one thing right after another and never give myself a break, I can burn out and find myself not enjoying the ride at all because all I am thinking about is how hard it is to breathe. Resting is important.

Opportunities that are visible to you may not always be the right one for you. I may be in a position to catch a wave (opportunity), but it still may not be the right wave for me. It may be the right wave for the person next to me. And if I see that other person get on that wave, I need to be excited for that person and the opportunity they were able to grab ahold of.

Helping your children navigate the opportunities of life is important to do as a father. One of the most powerful ways to train them up in this area is to set the example of what this looks like. And when opportunities are presented before you, explain to your children why you do or don't take the opportunity.

When Josh was in Kindergarten and Hannah was in second grade, they competed in Landsharks. It is a running club through their school that met after school on Mondays and Thursdays. I figured this would be a great fit for Josh. He really loves to run. Hannah enjoys running too, but I think Josh loves it the most. The first day of practice they did some running drills and then they played a game called sharks and minnows. A few kids on the team are the sharks and everyone else is the minnows. The sharks are in the middle of the field, while the minnows start at one end and have to run all the way to the other side without being tagged by the sharks. Those that are tagged also become sharks during the next round, so the shark pool gets larger each round and the minnow group gets smaller.

I was not surprised that Josh never got caught. Not only did he prove himself to be fast, but he also showed how smart he could be. As a minnow, he would wait until the other minnows began running out toward the sharks, then when the sharks would begin to close in and attack the oncoming minnows he would quickly run around the end and turn on the heat as he ran along the edge of the field for the safety zone. I was so proud of him. Because not only was he using his talent of being a fast runner, but he was also using his head and accomplishing something in a smart way. Too bad the other minnows didn't catch on to his strategy.

Conclusion

Our heavenly Father is the best Father there is. He is a Father who extends favor to His children so they can receive blessings in life. He showers them with affection so they never question how He feels about them. He leads them into truth so that no lie will ever keep them in bondage. He honors them to invest in them. He empowers them so that they are equipped and strengthened to accomplish what they are called to do. Finally, He reveals who His children are so that they never question their identity, but rather advance forward through life boldly.

As a father to your children, I hope and pray that you are encouraged by the example your heavenly Father has given you. If you will keep your dependence upon the Lord, let the Father's example be your plumb line, and pour into your children as a true FATHER, then you will see rewards beyond your wildest dreams. Enjoy every moment. Be a FATHER!

WHAT FATHER TEACHES

•He teaches kindness by being thoughtful and gracious even at home.

•He teaches patience by being gentle and understanding over and over.

•He teaches honesty by keeping his promises to his family even when it costs.

•He teaches courage by living unafraid with faith, in all circumstances.

•He teaches justice by being fair and dealing equally with everyone.

•He teaches obedience to God's Word by precept and example as he reads and prays daily with his family.

•He teaches love for God and His Church as he takes his family regularly to all the services.

•His steps are important because others follow.

Author unknown

Endnotes

1. U.S. Census Bureau, Children's Living Arrangements and Characteristics: March 2011, Table C8. Washington D.C.: 2011.

2. Osborne, C., & McLanahan, S. (2007). Partnership instability and child well-being. Journal of Marriage and Family, 69, 1065-1083

3. Matthews, T.J., Sally C. Curtin, and Marian F. MacDorman. Infant Mortality Statistics from the 1998 Period Linked Birth/Infant Death Data Set. National Vital Statistics Reports, Vol. 48, No. 12. Hyattsville, MD: National Center for Health Statistics, 2000.

4. Harper, Cynthia C. and Sara S. McLanahan. "Father Absence and Youth Incarceration." Journal of Research on Adolescence 14 (September 2004): 369-397.

5. Barber, Nigel. "Single Parenthood As a Predictor of Cross-National Variation in Violent Crime." Cross-Cultural Research 38 (November 2004): 343-358.

6. Teachman, Jay D. "The Childhood Living Arrangements of Children and the Characteristics of Their Marriages." Journal of Family Issues 25 (January 2004): 86-111.

7. Hendricks, C. S., Cesario, S. K., Murdaugh, C., Gibbons, M. E., Servonsky, E. J., Bobadilla, R. V., Hendricks, D. L., Spencer-Morgan, B., & Tavakoli, A. (2005). The influence of father print version/Fravel 83 absence on the self-esteem and self-reported sexual activity of rural southern adolescents. ABNF Journal, 16, 124-131

8. Bronte-Tinkew, Jacinta, Kristin A. Moore, Randolph C. Capps, and Jonathan Zaff. "The influence of father involvement on youth risk behaviors among adolescents: A comparison of native-born and immigrant families." Article in Press. Social Science Research December 2004.

9. National Longitudinal Survey of Youth.

10. Tillman, K. H. (2007). Family structure pathways and academic disadvantage among adolescents in stepfamilies. Sociological Inquiry, 77, 383-424.

11. Silk, Danny. Culture of Honor: Sustaining a supernatural environment. Destiny Image Publishers. 2009. p.160.

Made in the USA
Charleston, SC
16 January 2014